Tomorrow's Alphabet

By
George Shannon
Pictures by
Donald Crews

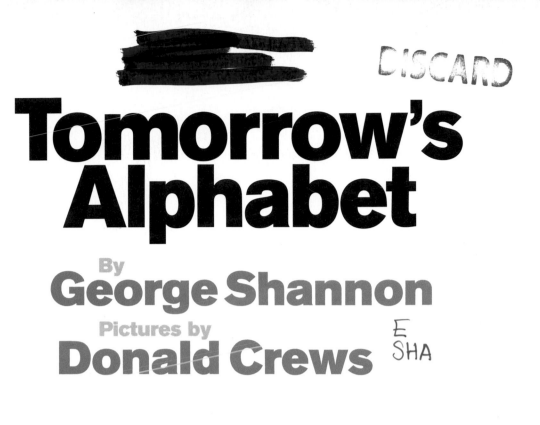

Greenwillow Books, New York

Watercolors were used for the full-color art. The text type is Akzidenz Grotesk.

Text copyright © 1996 by George W. B. Shannon Illustrations copyright © 1996 by Donald Crews All rights reserved. No part of this book may be reproduced or utilized in any form or by any means, electronic or mechanical, including photocopying, recording, or by any information storage and retrieval system, without permission in writing from the Publisher, Greenwillow Books, a division of William Morrow & Company, Inc., 1350 Avenue of the Americas, New York, NY 10019.

Printed in Hong Kong by South China Printing Company (1988) Ltd.

First Edition 10 9 8 7 6 5 4 3 2 1

Library of Congress Cataloging-in-Publication Data

Shannon, George. Tomorrow's alphabet / by George Shannon; pictures by Donald Crews. p. cm. ISBN 0-688-13504-8 (trade). ISBN 0-688-13505-6 (lib. bdg.) 1. English language–Alphabet– Juvenile literature. [1. Alphabet.] I. Crews, Donald, ill. II. Title. PE1155.S5 1996 [E]–dc20 94-19484 CIP AC

For **B**rian, **A**ndrew, and
Kaitlyn **S**hannon
–G. S.

For **A**nn, **N**ina, and **A**my,
and the **G**ang at **G**reenwillow
and **S**usan and **A**va (who put her foot in it)
–D. C.

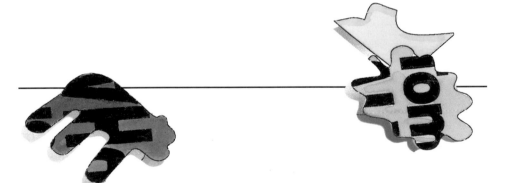

A is for seed—

tomorrow's

APPLE

B is for eggs—

tomorrow's

BIRDS

c is for milk—

tomorrow's

CHEESE

D 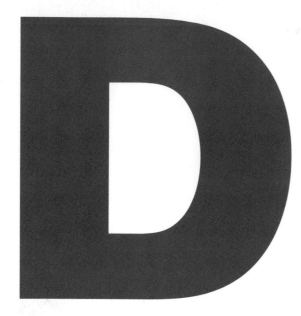 is for puppy—

tomorrow's

DOG

E is for campfire—

tomorrow's

EMBERS

F is for wheat–

tomorrow's

FLOUR

G

is for
bulbs–

tomorrow's

GARDEN

H is for yarn–

tomorrow's

HAT

is for water–

tomorrow's

ICE CUBES

J is for
pumpkin–

tomorrow's

JACK-O'-LANTERN

K is for
tomato–

tomorrow's

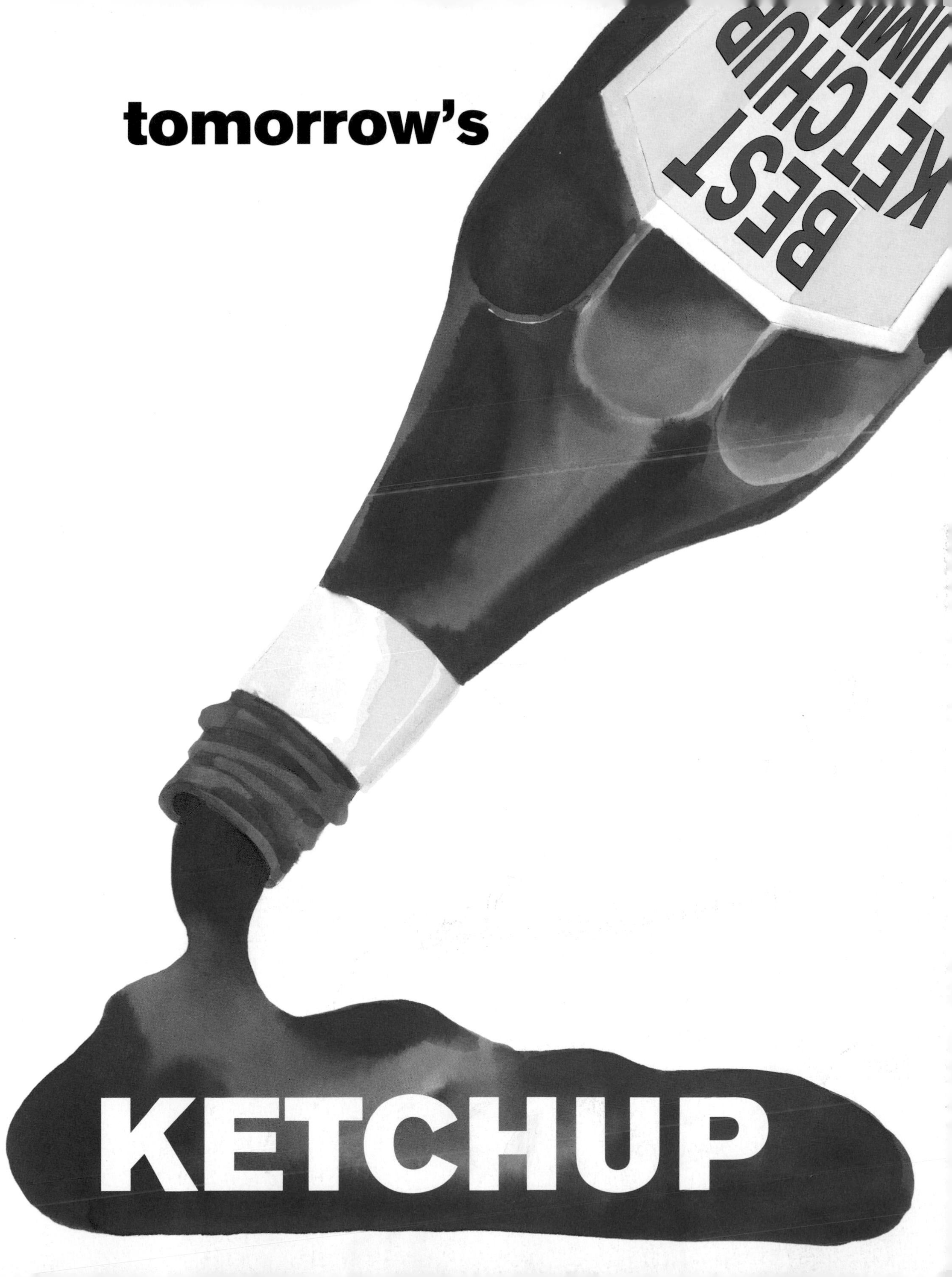

L is for bud–

tomorrow's

LEAF

M is for caterpillar–

tomorrow's

MOTH

N

is for twigs–

tomorrow's

NEST

O

is for
acorn–

P is for clay–

tomorrow's

POT

Q

is for scraps–

tomorrow's

QUILT

R is for grapes–

S is for vegetables–

tomorrow's

SOUP

T is for bread–

tomorrow's

TOAST

U is for stranger–

tomorrow's

US

V is for paper–

tomorrow's

VALENTINE

W

is for stones—

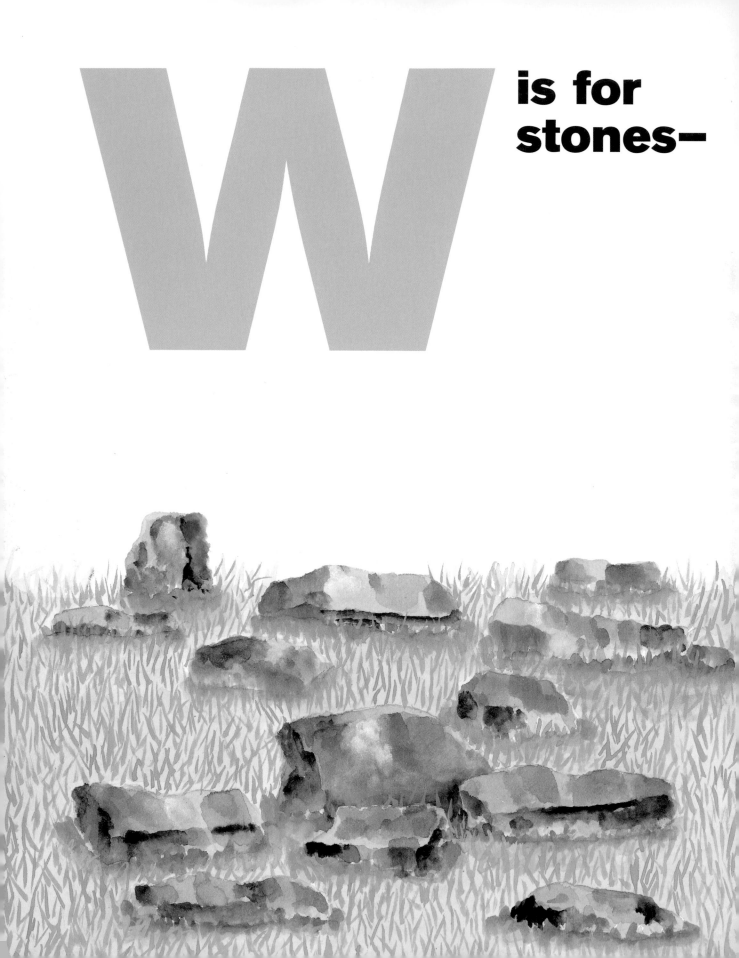

tomorrow's

WALL

X

is for bones—

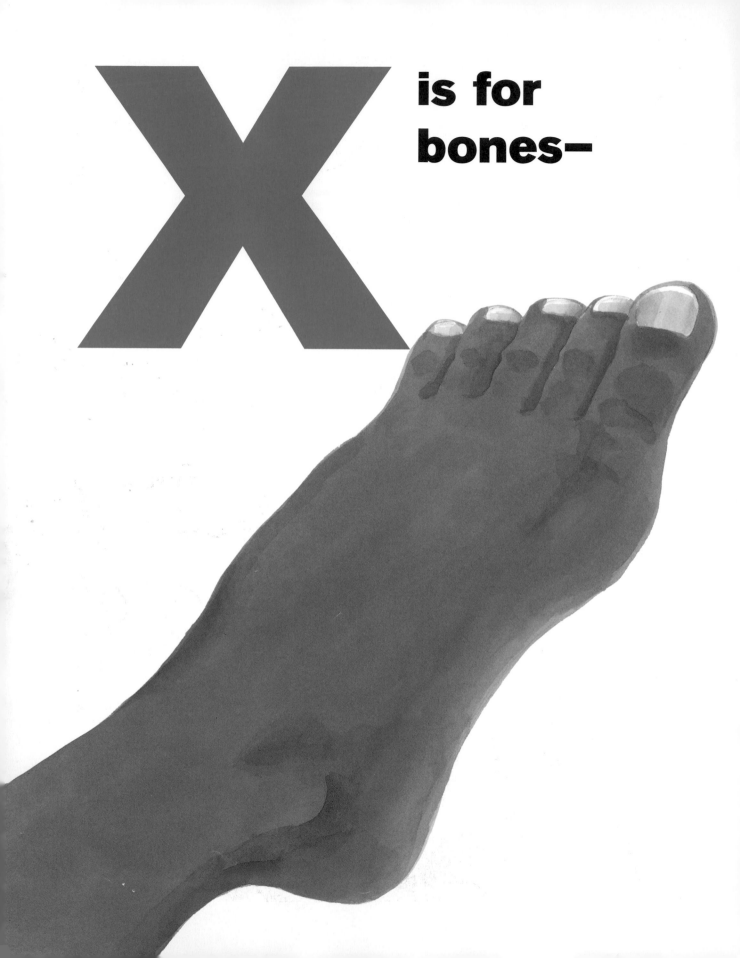

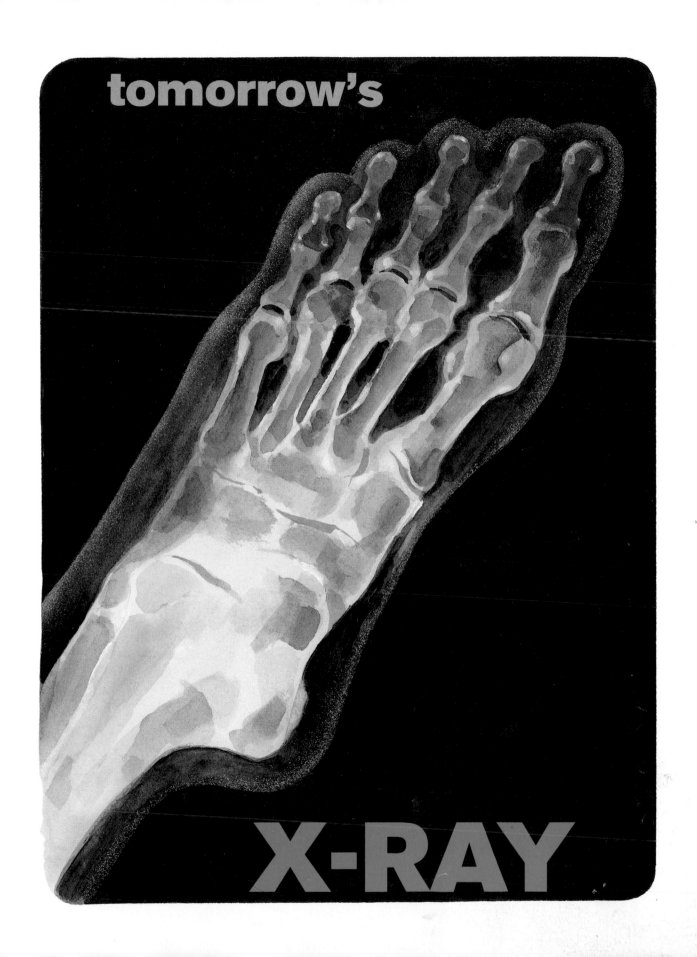

Y

is for sheep—

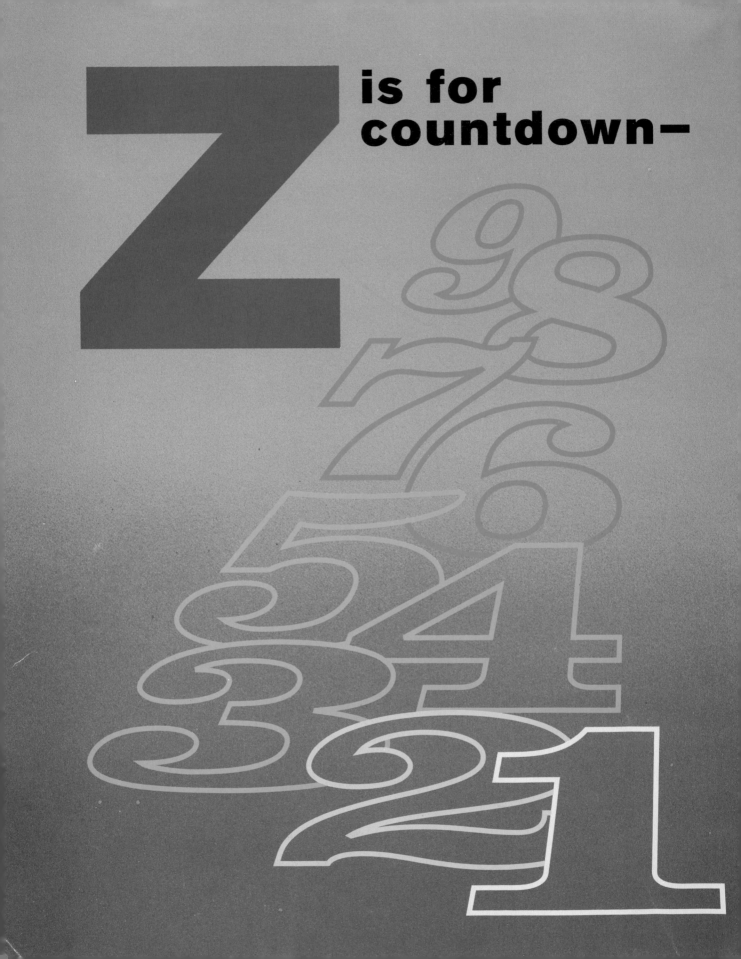

Z is for countdown—

9 8 7 6 5 4 3 2 1

tomorrow's

(0) ZERO